Thank You, Me

Ellie Oop

Balboa Press books may be ordered through booksellers or by contacting:

Balboa Press
A Division of Hay House
1663 Liberty Drive
Bloomington, IN 47403
www.balboapress.com
1 (877) 407-4847

ISBN: 978-1-9822-1942-0 (sc)
ISBN: 978-1-9822-1943-7 (e)

Library of Congress Control Number: 2019900141

Print information available on the last page.

Balboa Press rev. date: 01/30/2019

BALBOA
PRESS
A DIVISION OF HAY HOUSE

Dedication

This story is dedicated to my beloved, beautiful children, Meegan and David with love.

Acknowledgment

My heartfelt acknowledgement to Nancy Bo Flood, expert writer who was my dear mentor. Thank you.

Thank You, Me

WOO HOO! I'm awake!

And what do I see.

I see a new day.

OOOPS... I see something else!

My two hands pull covers

Clear up to my chin...

SQUEEZERS! I wave my two hands

And what do they do.

Wiggle my fingers

Feed me and dress me

Scratch all my itches

Rub all my ouches

Draw and paint pictures

And clap, clap, clap when I'm happy!

Thank you, My Hands, for all your care.

SQUINTS! I blink my two eyes

And what do they see.

Friends and new faces

My favorite fur babies

Peekaboo playmates

Colors and rainbows

Sunshine and starlight

And something wherever I look!

Thank you, My Eyes, for all you see.

TOOTLES! I feel my two ears

And what do they hear.

Stories and singing

Asking and answers

Woofing and mewing

Bee buzz and songbirds

Laughing and yelling

And everything quiet at night!

Thank you, My Ears, for all you hear.

SNONKERS! I see my wee nose

And what does it do.

Sniffs cookies baking

Smells flowers blooming

Sneezes and dribbles

Snorts loud at funnies

Maybe wears freckles

And snuffles soft toys when I'm sleeping!

Thank you, My Nose, for all your fun.

YUMMERS! I feel my wee mouth

And what does it do.

Licks jams and jellies

Giggles and snickers

Whispers and whistles

Puckers for kisses

Hollers, "That's funny!"

And says, "Please," "Thank you," "I love you!"

Thank you, My Mouth, for all your treats.

HUGGUMS! I see my two arms

And what do they do.

Hold tight to my hands

Bend into elbows

Cuddle my pillow

Carry my playthings

Wave high and wobble

And hug you hugging me!

Thank you, My Arms, for all your care.

DANGLES! I see my two legs

And what do they do.

Grab my feet tightly

Run me and hide me

Make me a lap place

Bend into knee bones

Jump when I holler

And climb into bed for my nap!

Thank you, My Legs, for all you do.

STUBBLES! I see my two feet

And what do they do.

Walk me and hop me

Skip and jump over

Feel warm in soft covers

Make my toes wiggle

And tickle to giggles

And dance me around and around!

Thank you, My Feet, for all your joy.

SMIDLINGS! I see my round middle

And what does it do.

Gives me my tummy

Feels my lungs breathing

Buttons my belly

Feels my heart beating

Cuddles my insides

And shapes me a bottom for sitting!

Thank you, My Middle, for all your comfort.

BONKEES! I feel my round head

And what does it do.

Soft hair in bunches

Eyes front for seeing

Wee nose right center

Chin for mouth's chewing

An ear stuck each side

And lots of sweet dreaming

Thank you, My Head, for being on top.

THUMPETS! I feel my hard bones

And what do they be.

Two arms and two legs

Ten fingers – ten toes

Two hips and some ribs

A neck and a backbone

My head stuck on top

And my joints bent into knobs!

Thank you, My Bones, for keeping me strong.

SMOOTHEES! I feel my soft skin

And what does it do.

Stretches and wrinkles

Comes in my color

Loves rubbings and scrubbies

Fits all my sizes

Tingles big goose bumps

And loves warming fur babies

Thank you, My Soft Skin, for loving to fit me.

TICKERS! I feel my heart beating

And what does it do.

Loves finding surprises

Loves sharing with friends

Loves playing silly

Loves helping others

Loves feeling happy

And loves hearing I love you!

Thank you, My Heart, for your loving care.

Thank you, Me, for all you do.

WOO HOO!

My ME is just like YOU!

Printed in the United States
By Bookmasters